You Can Draw Cartoons

Introduction

Throughout this book there are tips and advice on how to draw cartoons. There are suggestions for making up a cartoon story and ideas on how to keep a sketchbook. BUT the most important thing of all is to enjoy drawing.

📖 *Making a sketchbook*

One of the best ways to get really good at drawing cartoons is to keep a sketchbook.

👁 **Observe** – It is vital to look and listen to the world around you and record all the things you notice. This will be your store of ideas.

✍ **Key point** – Always carry your sketchbook with you. Draw people, places, animals and buildings. Draw everything that interests you. It might be useful to jot down things that you overhear people say. This will help when you are thinking of a story.

⭐ **Tip** – Cut out pictures from OLD magazines, label and file them. Then when you need to draw a picture, you will have good references.

Making a Start

To draw cartoons you need a pencil, a scrap of paper, a good imagination and that's it. But if you want to gradually build up a stock of useful materials, here are some suggestions.

⭐ **Tip**

Find a space where you can work. Make sure it has good light. Near a window is ideal. A drawing board isn't essential but it is good to have a clear table or desk. Maybe you can find a second-hand drawing board?

📖 Scrap deal

A collection of old envelopes, packing and scrap paper is very useful for doodling. Using scrap paper in this way means you don't have to worry too much about a cartoon going wrong and wasting an expensive piece of paper. The funny thing is that just knowing this can help you make a really fabulous drawing!

You can always paint over used envelopes and packaging with white paint to give yourself a cleaner surface to draw on. Leave some writing showing through as this can look exciting.

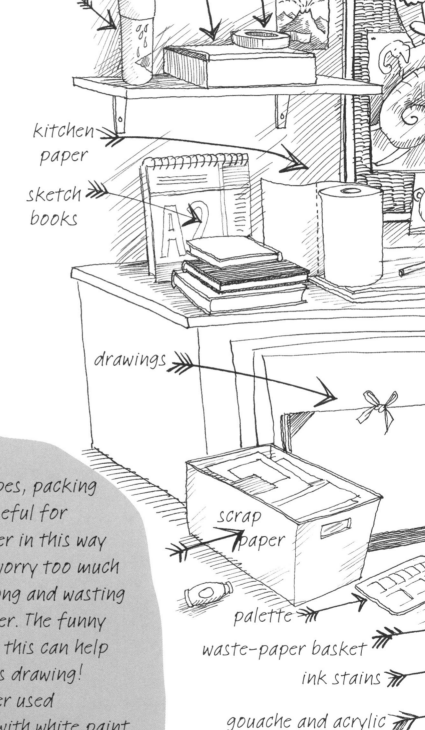

pin board

fixative

reference file

sticky tape

kitchen paper

sketch books

A2

drawings

scrap paper

palette

waste-paper basket

ink stains

gouache and acrylic

colouring pencils

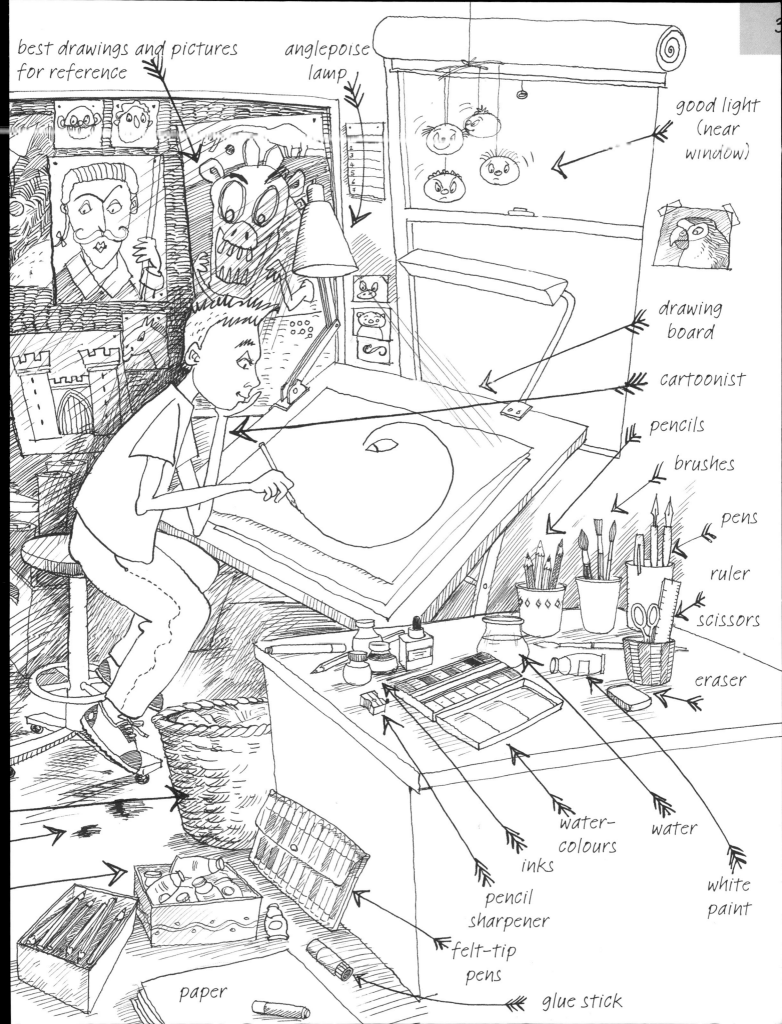

The Body

You will probably find it easier to start drawing your characters as pin-people.

☆ Tip

Don't forget to draw in the hips and shoulders.

👉 Key point

Here the proportions are as in real life but with cartoon characters the heads are usually drawn much bigger. Try this! Now flesh out your pin-men starting with sausage shapes or, if you feel confident enough, try adding clothes straight away.

📖 Body line up

Practise drawing cartoon people in a variety of different poses in your sketchbook. Remember, the more you practise drawing, the better you will get.

⭐ **Tip**

Try emphasising your character's qualities.

For example, a thin, tall person could have a thin, tall head and a fat, round person could have a fat, round head.

👉 **Key point**

Notice how the stripes on these characters' shirts help to emphasise their shape.

Heads

A good way to start drawing cartoon heads is to reduce them to a simple shape like an oval or square.

 Shape

This is a basic shape for the head and can be used for many cartoon characters.

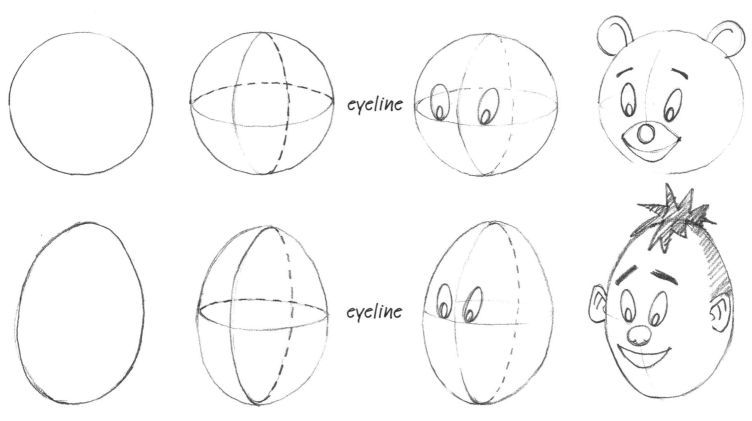

eyeline

eyeline

Draw a globe or an egg to start you off.

Divide this in half lengthways and note that the shape is 3D, not a flat circle or oval.

Draw in the eyeline which in real life would be roughly half of your globe but in cartoon life can be wherever you wish.

Now add the features.

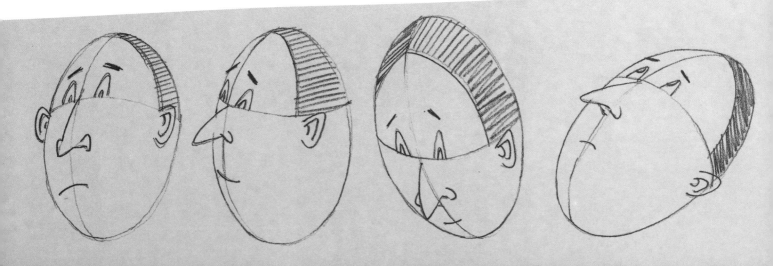

Key point

Notice how dramatically these faces change according to where in the shape their features are placed. With features at the top, our character has a large chin. When they are placed at the bottom, our character has a huge forehead! Experiment with this in your sketchbook.

Egg heads

Take an egg or table-tennis ball and draw on the two dividing lines – eyeline and lengthways – with a marker pen. Now draw your egg from many different viewpoints, looking up at it, down at it, sideways and so on. Add the features. This is great practice for drawing heads.

As your confidence grows, try making heads from different shapes.

Expressions

👁 *Observe*

Look at your own face in the mirror. Like an actor, practise a range of different expressions and try to draw them. Now pick a character you can draw and try to match his expression with a variety of different emotions. For example, on this page I have drawn a duchess character.

👉 *Key point*

Look at the opposite page. Notice how the hair is used to reinforce the expression. It is floppy and lank for 'tired', and jumping to attention for 'frightened'.

Clothes and accessories can be used in the same way to emphasise an emotion.
You can use body posture like this, too.

In this full-length portrait of the duchess, her expression is one of surprise. Notice how her earrings, handbag and tea cup are also caught in mid-action. This adds to the feeling of something having just happened. The white streak in the duchess's hair imitates a question mark.

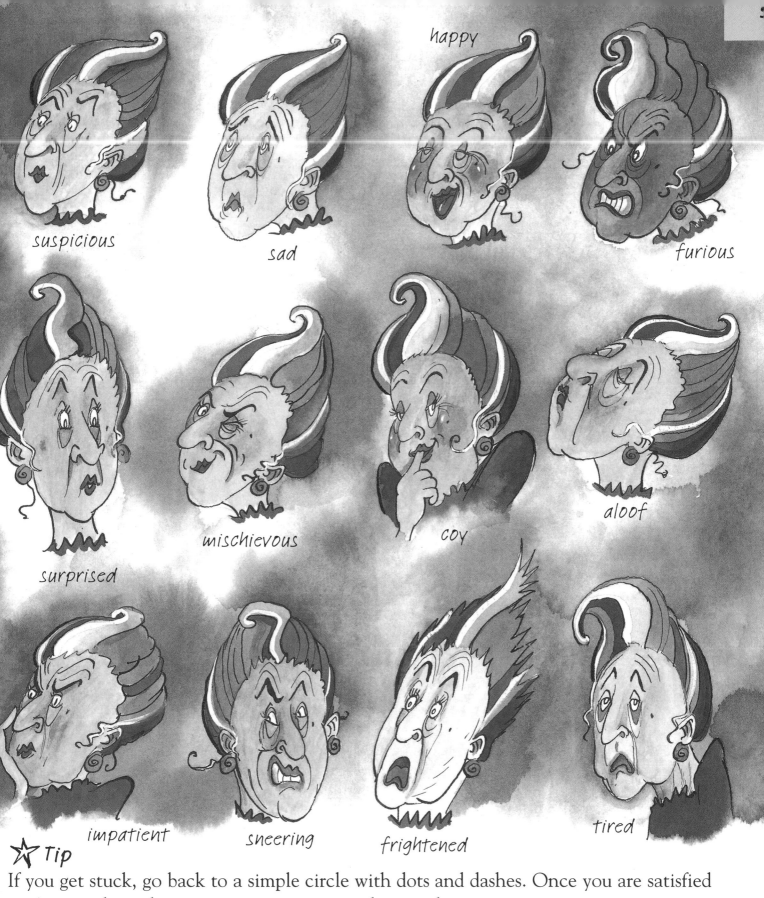

suspicious

sad

happy

furious

surprised

mischievous

coy

aloof

impatient

sneering

frightened

tired

⭐ Tip

If you get stuck, go back to a simple circle with dots and dashes. Once you are satisfied you've got the right expression, try again with your character.

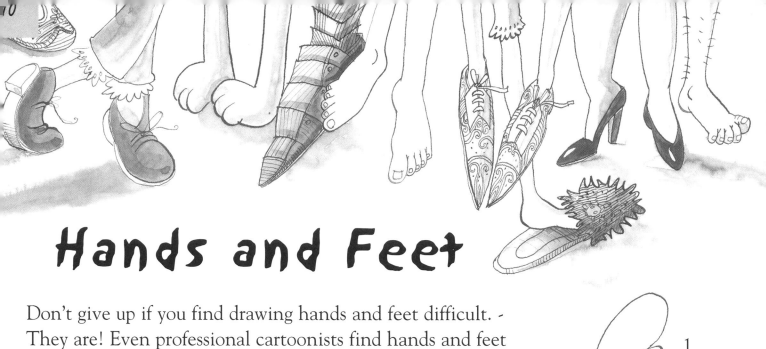

Hands and Feet

Don't give up if you find drawing hands and feet difficult. - They are! Even professional cartoonists find hands and feet difficult. Practise drawing from life as much as possible.

👁 Observe

For cartoon hands, don't attempt to draw all the lines on your hand. A few clear and simple marks will be easier to 'read'.

⭐ Tip

Your fingers are all different lengths. Look at your own hand.

Shape

Here are two ways to start drawing a hand:
1. Imagine the hand as a mitten. Then draw in the fingers.
2. Draw hands in the same way in which you might draw a pin-man - the bones first, then flesh out the drawing.

1

2

Key point

You can tell a lot about the character from the type of shoes they wear. So think carefully before dressing your cartoon characters. Their shoes may be dirty or extra shiny, big or small.

Well shod

Start a shoe sketchbook and fill it with drawings of people's shoes. Draw the shoes on and off the foot. If possible, make a rubbing or print of the shoe tread pattern as well.

Moving On

When drawing cartoon characters, ANYTHING GOES!

👁 Observe

Look at these simple characters. They are just like pin-men that have been filled out. Their facial features (eyes, nose) can be made up with dots and dashes or circles within circles.
You can practise by drawing these characters.
If you get stuck, turn back to the pin-man page.

Here the characters are walking, then running. For really fast running you can use speed lines like I've done or even add words like 'Whoosh' and 'Zoom'. They can be any colour and any shape, so use your imagination and create some really exciting characters.

★ Tip
For extra speed, draw your character running with his feet not touching the ground.

Cast of Characters

In the world of cartoon characters, stereotypes rule. A cartoon artist will probably wear a floppy hat, a smock, and hold an artist's palette with brushes. A real artist wouldn't walk around dressed like this but in cartoons you need to be able to identify the character quickly.

Here is a cast of characters for you to copy.

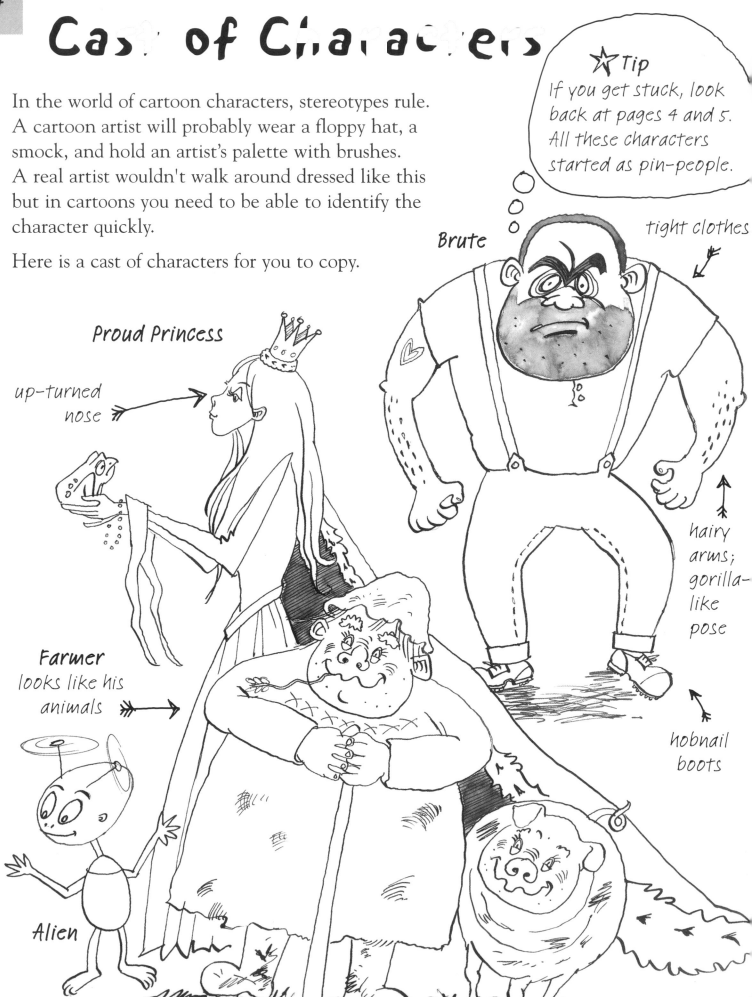

☆ **Tip**
If you get stuck, look back at pages 4 and 5. All these characters started as pin-people.

Brute

tight clothes

Proud Princess

up-turned nose

hairy arms; gorilla-like pose

hobnail boots

Farmer
looks like his animals

Alien

Mad Professor

large forehead
for big brain

bow tie

white
coat

book of
spells

check
trousers

odd
socks

**Old
Woman**

twinkly
eyes

sauced of milk
for puss

Wacky Witch

long finger nails

warts
on nose

bloomers

Rogues' gallery

As you gain confidence, try creating your own characters. Draw them in different positions and doing different things. Here are some more suggestions: Cut-throat Pirate, Circus Clown, Pop Idol, Film Star, School Cook.

Machines

You can make a cartoon character from anything, including machines.

Shape

To draw a car, start with
two rectangles. Add the wheels,
the doors and all of the details
like the lights and bumpers.
This is a good basis for any car.
For a fast car, make the shape long and thin.
For a slow car, tall and square is best.

☆ Tip

Use speed lines and angle the wheels to give
an impression of speed.

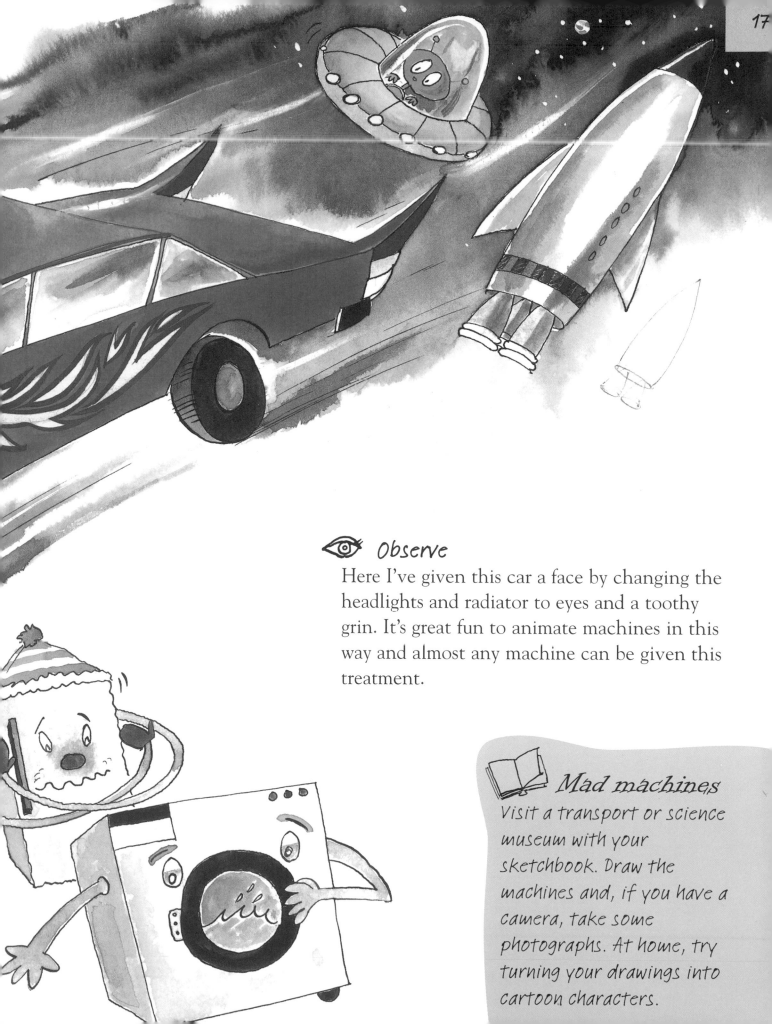

👁 Observe

Here I've given this car a face by changing the headlights and radiator to eyes and a toothy grin. It's great fun to animate machines in this way and almost any machine can be given this treatment.

📖 Mad machines

Visit a transport or science museum with your sketchbook. Draw the machines and, if you have a camera, take some photographs. At home, try turning your drawings into cartoon characters.

Cartoon Animals

You can usually start drawing cartoon animals with a simple shape like a circle, oval or triangle.

👁 Observe

Start the drawing of the dog with a circle for the head and an oval for the body. Finish this first stage with lines for legs and smaller circles for feet.

Shape

Gradually flesh out your drawing adding the ears, nose, eyes and tail. Finally, add any markings.

★ Tip

Remember, in cartoon world anything goes: your dog may walk on two legs; it may be orange, blue or purple; it may even ride a bike.

Dog

Cat   Bird   Mouse

 Reference zoo

Start a collection of animal pictures.
Cut out pictures from magazines or, better still, draw animals from real
life in your sketchbook. After a while you will have a useful reference
book to use as a source for your cartoons.

20

Here is a page of cartoon animals. Copy them and
let them inspire you to make up your own characters.
Once you can draw your cartoon character,
try drawing it with
different expressions.

⭐ *Tip*
The patterns on an animal's body
often help to show the shape.

Foreground

Once you are confident in drawing cartoon characters, you can set them in a scene or 'frame' and make a picture.

You can roughly break a picture into three separate areas or planes: the foreground, the middle ground and the background.

👁 Observe

The foreground means what is in front and, therefore, closest to us. You can use it to create drama and atmosphere and to show close-up expressions. The examples on this page show how to use the foreground.

👉 Key point

The foreground is very useful in cartoons to show emotions or surprise. The sudden 'cut' to a close-up makes the most of this dramatic moment.

☆ Tip

When making up the pictures in a story, don't overuse the foreground. An occasional close-up is much more effective.

Middle Ground

The middle ground is the most used of our three planes.
It is usually where the action takes place.
Here are some examples of how you might use the middle ground.

Setting the scene

Try making a simple concertina. Draw the background, side
pieces and proscenium to slot or stick in (see below).
This is like a mini theatre and you can play with the
background, middle ground and foreground and maybe
draw some characters. Finally, try making drawings from
the model in your sketchbook.

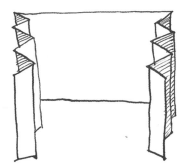

Background

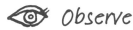

Background is important for setting the scene and for showing where the action is taking place.

Observe

Look at these drawings of a pin-man in the desert.

Notice how in (a) we feel that the pin-man is just setting out on his journey.

In (b) and (c) we guess that he is in the middle of the desert as the background seems to go on and on. But in (d) the feeling is that he is near the end and coming out of the desert. The only thing that is different in all of these boxes is the horizon line.

Where in the desert do you think he is in (e)?

Key point

The horizon line is very important.

It is an imaginary line showing where the sky joins the land. It can dramatically alter the mood and meaning of your cartoons.

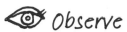 **Observe**

The background in this frame is important to set the scene for this story. The distant mountains, fields and path stretching from the house really help give the picture depth.

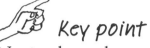 **Key point**

Notice how the use of the foreground in all these pictures adds to the atmosphere.

In all of these examples, notice how the three planes work together to create a great picture, full of atmosphere and drama.

Field trip

Take a trip to an art gallery and look at the paintings. How are the middle ground and background used in pictures? Try recording in your sketchbook those you find most interesting. You can do the same thing watching films on T.V. How do directors make their compositions exciting?

Comic Strips

The first thing you need is a story and this should be exciting or funny or maybe both. Don't make it too long or you won't leave enough room for the pictures.

Here are some suggestions for comic-strip stories. You can use these or make up your own.

BIG DOG - Alice's family buy a puppy but it cannot stop growing and growing and growing...

THE SEA SHELL GIRL - on holiday Pearl finds a sea shell but, as she discovers when her family return home, inside lives a tiny mermaid who must return to the sea.

AUNT RAT - Emily's aunt has a special trick. She can turn herself into a rat!

FLYING LENNY - Lenny wakes up to find he can fly.

THE VOYAGE OF THE EMERALD TIGER - Oliver stows away on board *The Emerald Tiger* as it sails in search of treasure and adventure.

Once you have the plot, you can create the characters. Practise drawing them in your sketchbook over and over again.

☆ Tip
You will need to make your characters look the same in each frame, so keep their features simple.

Key point
Do the comic strip in pencil first. Put in all of the speech bubbles. This is a great way to make sure everything fits and to deal with any problems before you spend ages on the finished comic strip. This is called a 'rough' or 'visual' and nearly all illustrators and cartoonists work like this.

Make your frames different sizes. It's more interesting. Look back at the pages on foreground, middle ground and background.

A sentence at the top of the frame can tell you the time or place, e.g. 'Four hours later...' or, 'Meanwhile, back at the ranch.'

It is easier to do the lettering first and draw the speech bubbles around after. Remember to put the speech bubbles in the order you want them to be read – from left to right. This is important because it may dictate where your characters need to be.
You can use thought bubbles as well as speech bubbles.

Draw the frame outlines with a ruler and pencil first BUT then draw over this guide in freehand.

Sound effects are a great way of making your story come alive.

Look at how all these are used in the story on the next page.

Caricature

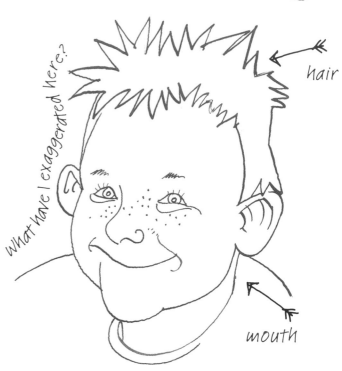

What have I exaggerated here?

hair

mouth

Making a caricature of someone is all about looking.
Look for a dominant feature that you can exaggerate, maybe a nose or eyebrows.

Key point

It is important that any information in your cartoon is understood clearly and quickly. To achieve this, simplify your drawings down to just the essential details. This way the reader can see instantly what you wish to communicate

Observe

Here I have caricatured a family friend as a Bassett hound! I did this, not only because her hair reminds me of a dog's ears but she actually owns two Bassett hounds. Look for chances like this when you are thinking how to caricature someone.

👁 Observe

Look and think carefully about the person you are caricaturing. Do they usually wear the same kind of thing or a particular colour? If so, dressing them in this will really help. Do they have a mannerism or habit you could include? They might like skateboarding so draw them with a skateboard or if they love music, draw them with a Walkman and musical notes.

Here are some examples of caricatures. What do they tell you about the 'victim'?

☆ Tip

Maybe you could draw them doing a favourite activity or job. Can you guess which of these is me? On the inside front cover there are some caricatures of the other people who have worked on this book!

📖 Mug shots!

Try caricaturing your family and friends, then test them on other members of your family to see if they know who it is. Tone down the exaggeration if they cannot tell who it is.

Top Ten Tips

⭐ Always carry your sketchbook and draw at every available opportunity.

⭐ Don't try to fit too much into each picture.

⭐ Look at your own face in the mirror to capture the expression you want.

⭐ Written sound effects can help to tell a story.

⭐ Always start with a thumbnail sketch before spending time on a larger finished drawing.

⭐ The simpler an image, the easier it will be to understand.

⭐ Keep scraps of paper to draw on. Sometimes the best drawings are made on the backs of envelopes.

⭐ Pin-people are a good way to start drawing cartoon figures.

⭐ If you are having trouble drawing something, look at the real thing.

⭐ When using speech bubbles, remember to leave enough space for the words.